TIMELESS IRELAND

TIMELESS IRELAND

Faces and Places of the Emerald Isle

Telefón

Photographs by Michael Rutherford

With text by Aubrey Watson

MetroBooks

MetroBooks

An Imprint of Friedman/Fairfax Publishers

©1998 by Michael Friedman Publishing Group, Inc.

Library of Congress Cataloging-in-Publication Data available on request

ISBN 1-56799-680-9

EDITOR: *Ann Kirby*
ART DIRECTOR: *Jeff Batzli*
DESIGNER: *Amanda Wilson*
PHOTOGRAPHY EDITOR: *Christopher C. Bain*
PRODUCTION MANAGERS: *Susan Kowal and Niall Brennan*

Color separations by Radstock Repro Ltd
Printed in England by Butler & Tanner Limited

10 9 8 7 6 5 4 3 2 1
For bulk purchases and special sales, please contact:
Friedman/Fairfax Publishers
Attention: Sales Department
15 West 26th Street
New York, NY 10010
212/685-6610 FAX 212/685-1307

Visit our website:
www.metrobooks.com

ACKNOWLEDGMENTS
The authors wish to thank the people of Ireland,
whose hospitality and kindness toward two strangers
made our work a pleasure.

DEDICATION
To my wife Debbie, and my sons Chad and Drew.
I have always been in awe of the wonder of creation, and have been
privileged to travel through it, capturing with my camera the work of our
Lord Jesus so that others may draw nearer to him and to the reality of his
presence in the world.

INTRODUCTION

Like so many Americans, Michael Rutherford and I can trace at least a part of our ancestry back to Ireland. The Irish have emigrated to the far reaches of the earth, settling down and embracing their new homes while always maintaining ties with their motherland. As a people, they reestablished themselves in new lands, and maintained their identity abroad like no other ethnic group. They celebrate their heritage in annual parades on Saint Patrick's Day, continue traditions of Irish music, and dive headfirst into civil service jobs and politics. The Irish stick together in their new homes, and have created a powerful voice in government, labor, and society. Their names—Kennedy, O'Connor, Ryan, Mulroony—can be found in abundance in any telephone directory in the English-speaking world, and often carry a great deal of power and prestige.

We journeyed to Ireland several times over the past two decades, not to trace our roots, but to gather photographs that would accurately and beautifully document the state of the country and its people. Yet as we traveled we found much more than beautiful landscapes, charming architecture, and smiling faces. As we roamed through the hills and valleys of this ancient, mystic land, we found ourselves embraced by the warmth of a people who have survived and maintained a unique national identity despite centuries of oppression, turmoil, and mass emigration.

The photos in this book are the culmination of several trips by car totaling more than four thousand miles (6,436km), the length and breadth of a country slightly smaller than the state of North Carolina. It is a visual journey from the west coast of the Dingle Penninsula to the northeast coast of Antrim, from County Mayo in the west to Wicklow and Waterford in the south and Dublin in the east.

We walked the hills where Saint Patrick carried his message in the fifth century, where Irish tenant farmers of years past worked the soil, and where thousands perished during the Great Potato Famine of the 1850s. We listened to the stories of the people we met, told in the chiming rhythm of their beautiful brogues, passed down in the traditional Gaelic tongue. Despite years of oppression under the iron fist of the British Empire, the Irish have held on to their language, their religion, their history, and their dignity.

Although we were seeking photos rather than relations, we were amazed by the familiar feelings that came over us in the villages and homes of the Irish families with whom we stayed. We spent many a damp evening in the parlors of Irish homes, warmed by glowing peat fires and the genuine hospitality of our hosts. One day, after hours of driving, we stopped to talk to two charming elderly gentlemen who were whitewashing the stone fence that lined the road in front of their cottage. After proper introductions, we were invited inside for a sip of poteen, a traditional home-brewed spirit

A dairy cow grazes on high ground alongside the rugged shore.

distilled from potatoes. We were encouraged to investigate our roots, to trace our ancestry through family and clan names, and were claimed as distant relatives by people we had just met.

We found such warm welcomes wherever we traveled in Ireland. We invite you, too, to join us on our journey. Come and soak up the rugged and poetic landscapes and lively urban and quiet rural life that inspired Ireland's great poets and authors, from James Joyce and William Butler Yeats to Seamus Heaney and Roddy Doyle. Visit the castles, monasteries, churches, and cemeteries of centuries ago, many of them standing unoccupied and undisturbed. Spend an afternoon in a village of thatched-roof houses and quaint shops, where the local butcher makes sausages and black puddings for traditional Irish breakfasts. Walk with us along the rugged sea coasts shrouded in mist to sheltered harbors where fleets of fishing boats wait to be unloaded. We will take you to the Crown pub in Belfast, and to Raftery's Rest, a cozy pub in Clare, for a pint or two by the fire. We'll watch the sun set on Galway Bay, and stroll alongside the Giant's Causeway on the Antrim Coast.

Michael Rutherford's brilliant photography will serve as your guide through this beautiful place, rich in history and charm, where the people are as enchanting as the landscape. *Céad míle fáilte.* One hundred thousand welcomes.

THE FACES OF A NATION

The faces of Ireland illuminate its unique history. The dominance of dark hair, fair skin, and light eyes reflects the heavily Celtic influence on the population, but centuries of intermingling—with French, Spanish, English, and even Viking blood—has given the Irish people a wealth of genetic diversity. Yet Irish faces can be surprisingly distinctive, bearing a variety of influences and remaining uniquely Irish just the same. These faces tell the history of a people, one that stretches from the green, rolling hills of Ireland all the way to the shores of North America, Australia, and beyond.

Just as the damp gray of Ireland's skies juxtaposes gracefully with the lush green of its hills and fields, the beaming smiles of Irish children are strikingly bright amid the often violent political upheaval that tears at the soul of this small nation. The spirit of the Irish—joyful, proud, sentimental, and wholly devoted to their homeland—resonates in young freckled faces. And as years go by, the smiles ingrain themselves, maturing beautifully into the calm, knowing grins of Ireland's distinguished elder men and women.

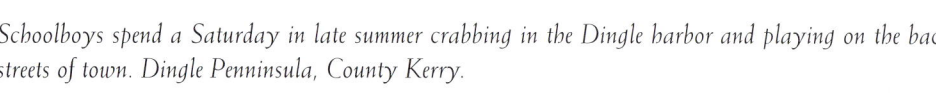

Schoolboys spend a Saturday in late summer crabbing in the Dingle harbor and playing on the back streets of town. Dingle Penninsula, County Kerry.

In Dublin, young people gather after school for a game of soccer, or to chat on street corners.

Patrons gather outside Fox's Pub in Glencullen, near Dublin, for an impromptu music session. Set high up in the Dublin Mountains, Fox's sits at a higher elevation than any other pub in Ireland. The slogan inside reads, "There are no strangers here—only friends who have not yet met."

OPPOSITE: *Newlyweds pose at Muckross House National Park, County Kerry.* ABOVE: *Married somewhat longer, the Dalys operate a townhouse bed and breakfast in the town of Wicklow.*

OPPOSITE: A patron enjoys a pint of stout by a warm turf fire at Raftery's Rest, a pub in County Clare named in honor of the blind Irish poet Anton Raftery. ABOVE: Every town and village has a victualler, or butcher, who prepares the meats displayed in the windows of his shop daily. Fresh sausages, puddings, and bacon are staples of traditional Irish breakfasts.

Terry Wilson is the owner of Raftery's Rest, a pub in County Clare.

Joe Dargan stands in the doorway of his sporting goods shop in the market town of Cashel, County Tipperary.

The crowd catches up on world events, County Sligo.

On a winding road between Killarney and Kenmare, County Kerry, sits a small creamery where local dairy farmers bring fresh milk each day. It's not unusual to see such goods transported the old-fashioned way.

OPPOSITE: Eddy Hutcheson builds traditional currachs: boats constructed of oak frames, covered with canvas (although leather was once used), and coated with pitch. In the fifth century, Saint Brendan the Navigator sailed to the New World in such a boat; the voyage was duplicated in 1976 by Tim Severing. Currachs are still used for in-shore sailing. Dingle Penninsula, County Kerry. ABOVE: A merchant seaman in Cork City's harbor. Cork is a bustling seaport, with ships arriving from and departing for cities all over the world every day.

OPPOSITE: A crewman aboard a tug at Cork City, the cultural and economic center of southwest Ireland. ABOVE: A crewman from the fishing fleet in Killybegs, a thriving fishing port in County Sligo.

ABOVE: With a smile on his face and a twinkle in his eye, this gentleman in Cork City stops long enough for a chat and a picture. OPPOSITE: A traditional weaver works the loom at Blarney Woolen Mills in County Cork.

OPPOSITE: *Seaweed is harvested along Ireland's coasts for use as fertilizer.* ABOVE: *Seán O'Farrell on the Sky Road, overlooking Clifden Castle, County Connemara.*

OPPOSITE: *Thomas Teirney raises sheep in a fertile valley at the foot of the Twelve Pins Mountains, in the western part of Ireland. ABOVE: Ireland is a country of green stitched together with stone fences. This one in Mamm Cross—the location of the classic film* The Quiet Man—*is in need of some repair.*

OPPOSITE: *Drawing water from a village well.* PAGES 37–38: *Sheila Flynn poses with the beautiful Irish landscape to her back and the wind in her hair.* ABOVE: *James Conlee, a farmer in Errisbeg, County Galway, takes a short break from his afternoon chores to chat.*

ONE HUNDRED THOUSAND WELCOMES

Céad míle fáilte. The motto is displayed all over Ireland and demonstrated regularly by the Irish people. In Gaelic it means "one hundred thousand welcomes." If hospitality has roots, they can surely be found in Ireland, a country with a long history of entertaining visitors. Even those who first set foot on Irish soil with the intent of conquering the small nation were eventually conquered themselves by the warm, welcoming spirit of the Irish people. The early Celts, the plundering Vikings, the English and the Scots—every group that came to Ireland settled right in, and stayed.

For many modern-day visitors to the Emerald Isle, a sojourn to Ireland is a trip to their ancestral homeland, for Ireland's greatest export has always been her people. Famine, political turmoil, and economic distress have sent countless Irish to establish new homes in America, Canada, Australia, and elsewhere. These émigrés proudly carried with them their Irish culture and heritage, and passed these on to their children and grandchildren. When first stepping foot on Irish soil, many foreign-born Irish find that the country is much as their parents or grandparents left it, ready to welcome them home with outstretched arms. The warmth of one hundred thousand welcomes echoes in every doorway, on every gate, beneath the hearth of every home, outside every pub, hotel, and inn. Ireland is waiting to welcome you, asking you to come in, sit a spell, perhaps listen to a story or two.

Vividly painted doorways are an Irish tradition.

Doors are painted a variety of colors throughout Ireland, but red appears to be a favorite, whether for grand town homes, like the one above, or whitewashed country cottages like the one at right.

OPPOSITE: Flowers abound in gardens and window boxes throughout Ireland. The smallest cottage garden is often a profusion of spring and summer hues. Flowers accent the soft pastel colors of many cottages, which are made of stone and coated with successive layers of whitewash made of quicklime. In years past tints were sometimes added to the whitewash in the form of iron oxide or other natural coloring agents; those traditional shades are still duplicated today. ABOVE: This cottage in the Limerick town of Adare is crowned by a classic thatched roof, many of which can still be found in Ireland. Thatch is an ideal roofing material for Ireland's climate, keeping the home warm in the cold, wet winter and cool in summer.

Bright flowers and a yellow gate are but a hint of the welcome awaiting travelers inside this bed and breakfast near Dingle, County Kerry.

Travelers are made to feel at home at bed and breakfast establishments throughout the country.

OPPOSITE: *Iron gates mark the entrance to the majestic government house in bustling Belfast.* ABOVE: *A quaint cobblestone path leads through the charming back streets of Dingle, County Kerry.*

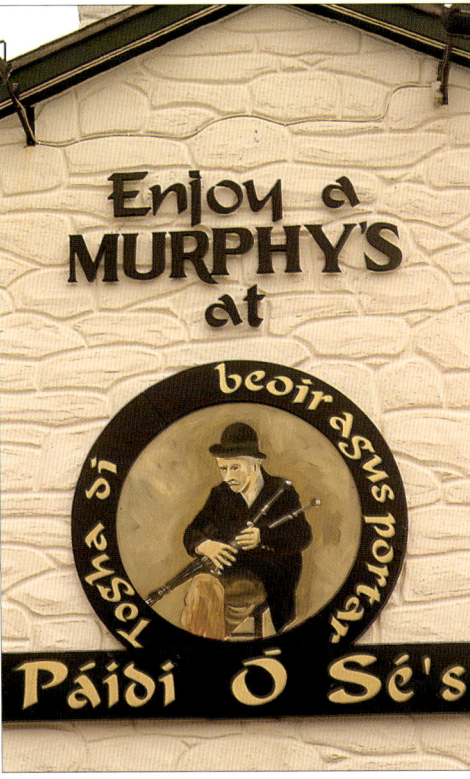

The pubs of Ireland are famous worldwide, and the signs that hang outside entice visitors with promises of live music, good food, and draught stout.

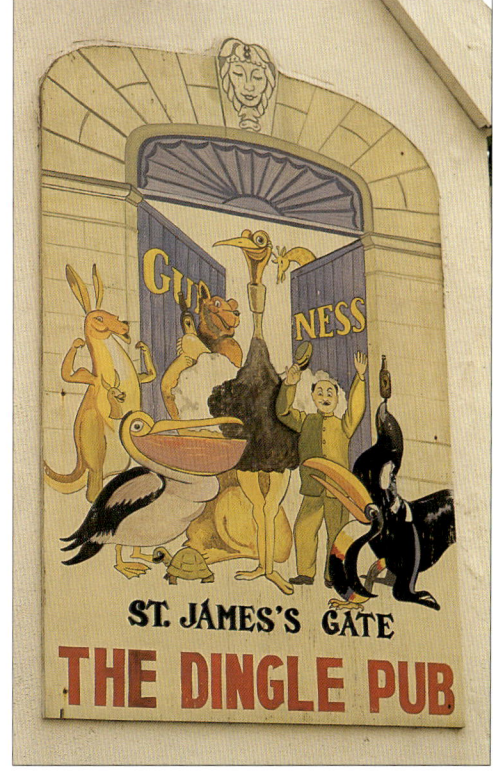

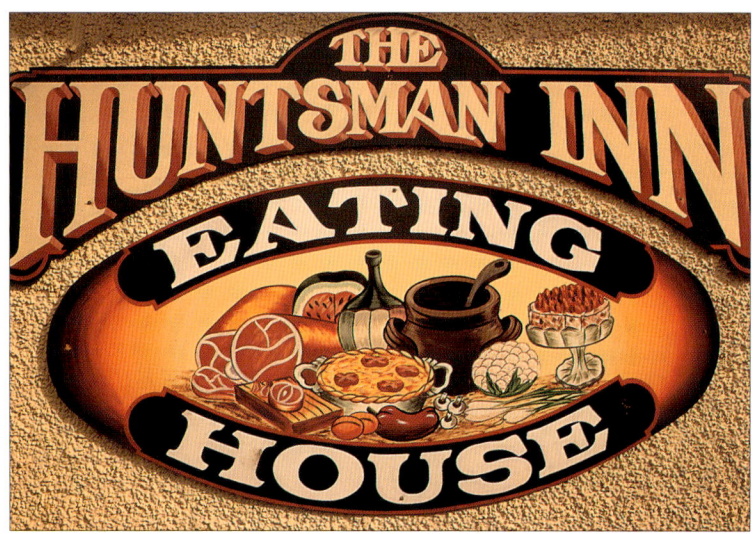

Signs outside many Irish shops and pubs are handpainted by local artisans, and even mass advertising often has a vintage feel.

GRAVESTONES OF HISTORY

Religion is, and has always been, a matter of some importance in Ireland. While the Roman Catholic church remains dominant in Ireland, especially in the Republic, the people of Ireland demonstrated a strong spirituality long before Saint Patrick converted the wild, pagan Celts. Ancient Druids worshipped on sites that were deemed sacred for centuries by their prehistoric predecessors. Likewise, as the Irish became Catholic, they adapted many of the sacred rites, myths, and places of their Celtic ancestors to suit their new-found faith.

The Church's influence on Ireland's history and spirit has been formidable from the beginning. Saint Patrick alone is credited with founding more than 300 churches, and baptizing 120,000 people. When most of Europe plunged into the Dark Ages after the fall of the Roman Empire, Irish civilization and scholarship entered what is believed by many to be its golden age. Mastering the art of illumination, Irish monks transcribed not only religious texts but also preserved Ireland's rich mythology, which had been passed from generation to generation in the oral tradition. Yet this golden age did not endure for long, and in the centuries since, the Irish have fought hard to express their faith. When Viking invaders sacked Ireland in the eighth and ninth centuries, they attacked not only the castles of the nobility, but also the monasteries, where kingly treasures were kept. Later on, from the time of the Reformation until the nineteenth century, Catholicism was forbidden by the ruling British. This resulted in the destruction or conversion of many Catholic churches, and prohibited the construction of new ones.

Each invasion, each struggle, each age of Irish history has left its mark upon the landscape, and the shadows of Ireland's past and present affect the scenery as deeply as they do the Irish soul. Small country churches, ancient cemeteries, and the ruins of castles, monasteries, and fortresses dot the Irish countryside as reminders and mementos of what has come before, like gravestones of history.

OPPOSITE: Dunluce Castle, on the Antrim Coast near Portrush in Northern Ireland, dates to the fourteenth century. It was abandoned in 1641, after the kitchen portion of the structure fell into the sea during a storm, taking a number of the household staff to their deaths.
FOLLOWING PAGES:
The ruins of a thirteenth-century Dominican friary sit at the foot of the Rock of Cashel, County Tiperrary, where Saint Patrick once preached.

A Norman tower and the remains of a castle in the countryside are invaded now only by birds and an occassional traveler.

These towers are of two distinctly different styles, which can be attributed to the times in which they were built, as well as to the purposes they served.
Many towers were built during the Viking invasions, when they acted as watchtowers and defensive bases.

Belfast Castle was completed in 1870, the last of several castles built on the site since the Normans constructed the first Belfast Castle there in the twelfth century. The castle was presented to the City of Belfast in 1934, and is now open to the public.

Towers along Ireland's coasts were sometimes used as lighthouses.

The grounds of the Blarney estate as seen from the top of Blarney Castle, built in 1446. Legend has it that anyone who kisses the Blarney Stone, a large outcrop atop the castle, will be given the gift of eloquence.

OPPOSITE: *Round castle towers provided panoramic views of approaching enemies, as well as protective cover for archers on the roofs. Entries were placed two or three stories off the ground, ladders were pulled inside when invaders approached. ABOVE: Clifden Castle in County Connemara was the home of John D'Arcy, who founded the town of Clifden in 1815. FOLLOWING PAGES: Doe Castle in northwest Ireland was built in the fifteenth century, and rebuilt in the nineteenth.*

An ancient Celtic verse reads:
    "God grant us peace and joyful love
    And may the face of Heaven's King
    Beam on us when we leave behind
    Our bodies blind and withering."

The customs house in Dublin. The figure atop the dome represents hope.

St. Soman's Cathedral, Cobh, County Cork.

OPPOSITE: "Deck of cards" houses line the street in front of St. Colman's Cathedral in Cobh. Called Queenstown when Ireland was under British rule, the city reverted to its Irish name—pronounced "cove" and meaning "haven" in Irish—when the Republic was formed. From this port city, countless Irish people sailed for America during the famine. Cobh was also the last port of call for the ill-fated Titanic, which was built in the Belfast shipyards. ABOVE: Churchyard gates, Northern Ireland.

OPPOSITE AND ABOVE: *Ancient Celtic motifs decorate many Irish graves.* PAGE 76, TOP: *A cottage on Ireland's rugged southwest coast, its original thatched roof long ago replaced with slate, has endured many Atlantic storms.* PAGE 76, BOTTOM: *Dunbeg fort was built during Ireland's Iron Age, sometime between 500 B.C. and 500 A.D.. It sits on a cliff at the base of Mount Eagle, overlooking Dingle Bay.* PAGE 77: *Kylemore Abby was built in the nineteenth century as a private home for an English shipping magnate. It is now a girls' boarding school, and a popular attraction in County Connemara.*

The cemeteries of Ireland are as picturesque as the landscape, and Irish tombs reflect pious Catholicism combined with ancient Celtic art.

FROM FARMLAND TO CITY

There is a sense of continuity that runs through the cities, towns, and villages of Ireland, connecting modern life to both recent and ancient history. Pre-Christian Ireland was divided into almost 150 kingdoms, known as *Tuatha* (which means, simply, "people"), all ruled over by a High King. As the nation converted to Catholicism, monasteries were founded based on the old *Tuatha*, and diocesan maps were drawn based on ancient clan divisions. The churches, abbeys, and castles of the ancient kings were the centers around which most of Ireland's small towns and villages were built, and today, the parish church remains the cornerstone of local life throughout rural Ireland. Much as they have for centuries, townspeople and farmers from surrounding areas congregate at the pubs, inns, and shops that flourish in these tight-knit communities.

Similarly, Ireland's history is etched in the landscapes of its cities, and even these thriving urban centers retain many ties to the nation's mythic past. It is the cities that bear the bulk of the scars—old and new—from Ireland's endless struggle with England. Dublin was the site of the 1916 Easter Rising (which led to the establishment of the Irish Free State in 1922, and later the Irish Republic), and numerous public monuments in modern Dublin pay homage to the patriots who secured this freedom. In the north, Belfast prospered during the nineteenth century, when some of the greatest ocean liners ever built were constructed in her shipyards. This prosperity was a key reason behind Britain's attachment to Ulster, and modern-day Belfast—the seat of government in Northern Ireland—remains a bustling industrial center surrounded by fine neighborhoods. But the painful conflict between Catholics and Protestants in Belfast and the surrounding areas has torn at the heart of the city, and the entire nation. And while successful peace talks offer hope, the wounds of this seemingly endless war will undoubtedly take time to heal.

A lamb stands against the dramatic backdrop of the Galway coast.

OPPOSITE: *A thatched-roof windmill, County Wexford.* ABOVE: *Schoolchildren enjoy an outing in County Antrim.*

Idyllic country scenes are to be found throughout Ireland.

When asking for directions in Ireland, locals will often tell you that your destination is just "down the road a piece."
In rural areas, you might find yourself traveling down the road for over a mile.

OPPOSITE: *Old schoolhouse, Northern Ireland. ABOVE: Ireland is known as a sheep country, and is famous for its fine woolen sweaters.*

Stones attached to ropes hold down a thatched roof against strong Atlantic winds. A popular Irish saying is, "Ní bí lá gaoithe lá na scoilbe," which means, "the day of the gale is not the day for thatching."

Cutting turf. Turf is used as a source of heat in many Irish homes and public places. Turf produces very high heat with little smoke and a small flame, and produces a pleasing, unforgettable aroma.

OPPOSITE: Feeding time on a farm in County Mayo. ABOVE: Although farming remains a common livelihood, the Irish countryside is dotted with abandoned farmhouses.

OPPOSITE: *Ireland's climate is comfortable year-round. An abundance of rain results in lush gardens and ivy-covered walls. ABOVE: Irish rural cottages are small but comfortable, and the sparse but cozy ambience has given rise to an "Irish country" decorating style around the world.*

OPPOSITE: *Potatoes, once a mainstay of the Irish diet, remain a popular crop and staple food. ABOVE: A farmer in Northern Ireland returns from a long day in the fields.*

OPPOSITE: An old Irish proverb says, "A wild goose never reared a tame gosling." ABOVE: Inside a country cottage in Dingle, County Kerry.

Sunset on Galway Bay.

A reproduction of a Viking boat.

Harvested peat awaits loading for the market.

ABOVE: Wheelbarrows loaded with peat are a common sight outside many old cottages. FOLLOWING PAGES: Giant's Causeway, on the Antrim Coast. Legend has it that the giant Finn MacCool threw down these stones to create a walkway between Ireland and Scotland.

Ireland is an island nation with thousands of miles of shoreline and hundreds of seaside towns and harbors, each possessing a post-card view.

OPPOSITE: *A derelict boat at low tide in Galway.* ABOVE: *Twin church spires of Clifden in County Connemara. This little town bustles each August during the famous Connemara Pony Show.*

Tourism is a major industry in Ireland. This fellow, dressed in period costume, offers visitors a glimpse of Irish urban style in the days of James Joyce and Oscar Wilde.

A peaceful street scene, typical in a quiet Irish village.

The conflict in Northern Ireland is complicated, and emotions run high on both sides. The pain and suffering of both factions are reflected in murals painted on buildings in a working-class neighborhood of Belfast.

The conflict in Northern Ireland divided the population between Catholics seeking religious freedom and Protestants loyal to the British crown. One woman in Northern Ireland told us,"I am Irish through and through, but I'm a British subject."

ULSTERS·PAST·DEFENDERS

1970
~
1992

WE WIL

1920

1970

OUR F

NA

UDR

'B'SPECIALS

WHO WILL DEFEND ULSTER NOW?

OPPOSITE: *An Irishman in an antique car makes his way to a parade in Northern Ireland.* ABOVE: *Peacetime in Belfast. A child enjoys a sunny day aboard a makeshift swing in the Catholic part of town.*

ABOVE: *War memorial, Belfast. OPPOSITE: Bicycles are a popular means of transportation in Ireland, and some have been in use for a long time.*

THE LURE OF IRISH LIFE

Despite the breathtaking landscapes and historic sites, Ireland remains a place that must be more than just seen—it must be experienced. A trip to Ireland is more than a sightseeing tour; it is a journey for all the senses. From quiet strolls along the shore to rough-and-tumble Gaelic football matches, the attractions of Irish life are as diverse as they are rich and enjoyable. No trip would be complete without a few days spent fishing along the Dingle Penninsula, a few evenings spent socializing by the peat-burning fire at a village pub, or dancing to the traditional reels and jigs of local musicians at a church céilí. The lush green landscapes lend themselves well to long rounds of morning golf, and the quiet still waters of Ireland's inland lakes are often parted by the carefully timed paddling of teams of rowers. It is, in many ways, just as it has always been, a land of timeless beauty, ageless wonder, and hopeful people.

Since ancient times, this magical, mythical, mysterious land has been personified as a woman: a goddess, a female warrior, a loving mother. Now, Ireland calls her lost children home, and beckons foreigners to investigate her beauty. She lures them with warm welcomes, enchanting music, and daring adventures, and such charms are both persuasive and ageless. As William Butler Yeats wrote (translating from a fourteenth-century poem):

"I am of Ireland,
And the Holy Land of Ireland,
And Time runs on," cried she.
"Come out of charity,
Come dance with me in Ireland."

Fly fishing on a Saturday,
County Kerry.

Fishing for trout near Innishfree in County Sligo, often called "Yeats Country." "I hear lake water lapping with low sounds by the shore," wrote Yeats in the poem "Innishfree."

OPPOSITE: *The sign tells it all, County Antrim. ABOVE: Gentle streams of cold gin-clear water flow through the Irish countryside.*

Fishing with Eddie Daly in Lough Bleagh, near Adare in County Kerry. An instructor of river angling, he teaches shooting and archery as well.

Angling for salmon with fly tackle—a skill and an art.

Countless streams and rivers that offer fine fishing opportunities flow through the towns and villages of Ireland.

A sculling team practices in the harbor in Cobh, County Cork.

A fishing boat sits high and dry at low tide on the northwest coast.

Monk's, a cozy little pub in Ballyvaughn, where guests can enjoy traditional music three nights a week.

The warm hearth and comfortable atmosphere makes Raftery's Rest a favorite gathering place.

OPPOSITE: *Like many small-town pubs, the Laurels in Killarney offers rooms or apartments to let overhead.* ABOVE: *The Crown Liquor Saloon in Belfast is one of the oldest pubs in Ireland. Established in the late nineteenth century, the Crown is operated today by the National Trust. The private cubicles are called "snugs."*

Bikes are a popular mode of transporation through the Irish countryside. Tourists can rent bikes at places like The Súgán in Killarney.

Fox's Pub in the Dublin Mountains specializes in fresh seafood and traditional music.

OPPOSITE: *A group of school children tour a historic village near Belfast.* ABOVE: *Gaelic football looks like soccer, but that's where the resemblance ends. It is a rough-and-tumble sport and the rules, it is said, are always subject to change. Gaelic football attracts the largest crowds of any sport in Ireland.*

The lush green Irish landscape lends itself perfectly to the sport of golf, and the Irish pursue it passionately. There is a higher percentage of golfers in Ireland than in any other country in Europe. This beautiful course is on the Antrim Coast.

OPPOSITE AND ABOVE: *Horse racing, hurling, football, and golf are all watched and played with a passion in Ireland. A day of golf offers a good excuse to spend time in the enchanting Irish countryside. Some of the most challenging and lovely golf courses are in western Ireland, such as this one in Enniscrone, County Sligo.*

Patrick Manske takes a break from traffic on a Saturday afternoon in Killarney.